Real-Life Superpowers

BRAVERY IS A SUPERPOWER

by Mari Schuh

PEBBLE
a capstone imprint

Published by Pebble, an imprint of Capstone
1710 Roe Crest Drive, North Mankato, Minnesota 56003
capstonepub.com

Copyright © 2024 by Capstone. All rights reserved. No part of this publication may be reproduced in whole or in part, or stored in a retrieval system, or transmitted in any form or by any means, electronic, mechanical, photocopying, recording, or otherwise, without written permission of the publisher.

Library of Congress Cataloging-in-Publication Data is available on the Library of Congress website.
ISBN: 9780756576608 (hardcover)
ISBN: 9780756576554 (paperback)
ISBN: 9780756576561 (ebook PDF)

Summary: A new neighbor moves in across the street. You say hello, even though you're nervous. You make a mistake but tell the truth. Being brave means doing the right thing, even though it can be hard. Learn more ways you can show bravery every day and use your superpower to help everyone around you!

Image Credits
Getty Images: Andersen Ross Photography Inc, 18, BJI/Blue Jean Images, 19, by Alfian Widiantono, 10, DaniloAndjus, 7, Gravity Images, 13, iStock/Onfokus, 11, iStock/SolStock, 5, kali9, 14, 16, LWA/Dann Tardif, 17, PM Images, 8; Shutterstock: Inside Creative House, 9, Ivonne Wierink, 21, Kapitosh, design element (background), Sergey Novikov, Cover, Sunflower Light Pro, 15, UfaBizPhoto, 6, VLADIMIR VK, 20, wavebreakmedia, 4

Editorial Credits
Editor: Alison Deering; Designer: Bobbie Nuytten; Media Researcher: Rebekah Hubstenberger; Production Specialist: Whitney Schaefer

All internet sites appearing in back matter were available and accurate when this book was sent to press.

Printed and bound in China. PO 5593

Table of Contents

Bravery Matters 4

Bravery at Home 10

Bravery at School 14

Helping Others 18

    Bravery Bracelets 20

    Glossary 22

    Read More 23

    Internet Sites 23

    Index 24

    About the Author 24

Words in **bold** are in the glossary.

Bravery Matters

When was the last time you were brave? Did you face your fear of swimming? Maybe you went to summer camp for the first time. How did it feel to be brave?

Bravery means doing hard things, even when you are scared. It means doing the right thing, even though it is hard to do.

Bravery is a **superpower**. When you do hard things, you learn to believe in yourself. This gives you **confidence**. You make good choices, even though you are afraid. Trying new activities helps you learn and grow.

Sometimes people are not brave. They might feel fear or **anxiety**. They might not stand up for what is right. They might worry people will tease them. They might be afraid to make a **mistake**.

It is okay to feel scared. Sometimes fear can keep us from trying fun, new things. Other times fear can keep us safe. We might be scared of something because it is dangerous. We do not want to be unsafe. We want to make smart choices.

Bravery at Home

You can be brave at home. Is your dad making a new meal for supper? Eat a few bites. You might really like it!

Do you have a new neighbor? You can be brave, even if you feel **shy**. Think about a time you were brave. Remember that you can do hard things! Say hi to your neighbor. Bring them some treats. They might become your friend!

Ammar is learning to in-line skate. But he is scared. Learning new things is not easy! It takes **patience** and **practice**.

Taking small steps is a smart way to be brave. Instead of going to the busy park, Ammar skates in his garage. He takes short breaks. He feels safe.

Bravery at School

Gabe is scared to start a new school. He doesn't know much about it. Learning more will help Gabe be brave. He takes a school tour. He learns where his classroom is. Being prepared helps Gabe feel better.

Being brave at school helps you be a good friend. Is a classmate being **bullied**? You can do the right thing, even if it is scary. Tell yourself that you can do hard things. You can be brave and stand up for your classmate.

Alex is having a tough time learning his spelling words. He feels anxious. Alex takes a break. He is **mindful** of his body. He closes his eyes. He takes slow, deep breaths.

Alex starts to feel **calm**. Now he can study again. He shows bravery by doing his best. He keeps trying and does not quit.

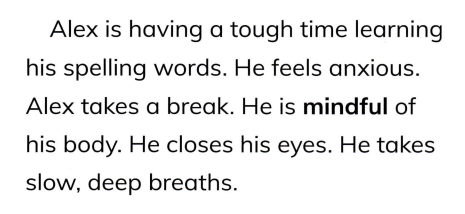

Fumi put a pen into the pencil sharpener. Now it is broken. She wants to go to recess to play with her friends. But she chooses to be brave. She tells her teacher the truth. She says she is sorry.

Helping Others

You can help other people be brave too. How? People see you facing your fears. They watch you try new things and learn new skills. They might decide that they can be brave just like you. They learn that they have this superpower too!

Bravery Bracelets

Remembering times you were brave can help you the next time you feel scared. Make this fun craft as a way to remind yourself just how brave you are!

What You Need

- sheets of paper
- scissors
- pencil, pen, crayon, or marker
- tape

What You Do

1. Cut a sheet of paper into long, thin strips.

2. Think of a few times when you were brave. Write about what you did on the strips of paper.

3. Roll the strips of paper into circles and tape them to create bracelets.

4. Soon, you will have many bravery bracelets. You can even link the bracelets together to make a chain of courage.

5. Acts of bravery really add up! Look at your bravery bracelets the next time you need to be brave. Remind yourself that you can do hard things!

Glossary

anxiety (ang-ZYE-uh-tee)—a feeling of worry or fear

bully (BUL-ee)—to be mean, scare, or pick on someone

calm (KALHM)—quiet and peaceful

confidence (KON-fuh-duhns)—to trust in a person or thing

mindful (MIND-full)—being aware of your body, mind, and feelings in the present moment

mistake (muh-STAKE)—something done in the wrong way

patience (PAY-shuntss)—staying calm and respectful while waiting or dealing with problems

practice (PRAK-tiss)—to keep working to get better at a skill

shy (SHYE)—not feeling comfortable around other people

superpower (soo-pur-POW-ur)—an important skill that can affect yourself and others in a big way

Read More

Blevins, Wiley. *Be Brave!* Egremont, MA: Red Chair Press, 2021.

Lindeen, Mary. *Feeling Brave.* Chicago: Norwood House Press, 2022.

McAneney, Caitie. *Sometimes We Feel Afraid.* New York: Cavendish Square Publishing, 2022.

Internet Sites

Inspire My Kids: Great Quotes About Bravery and Strength for Kids
inspiremykids.com/quotes-bravery-kids/

KidsHealth: Kids Talk About: Feeling Scared
kidshealth.org/en/kids/comments-scared.html

Sesame Workshop: Bravery Badges
https://sesameworkshop.org/resources/bravery-badges-veterans/

Index

activities, 4, 6, 12
anxiety, 8, 16

bullying, 15

confidence, 6

fear, 5, 8, 9, 18

meals, 10
mindfulness, 16
mistakes, 8

neighbors, 11
new schools, 14

safety, 9
saying sorry, 17
skating, 12
summer camp, 4
swimming, 4

teasing, 8
telling the truth, 17

About the Author

Mari Schuh's love of reading began with cereal boxes at the kitchen table. Today she is the author of hundreds of nonfiction books for beginning readers. Mari lives in the Midwest with her husband and their sassy house rabbit. Learn more about her at marischuh.com.